# UNRA

# Daddy's Shadow:

## A DAUGHTER'S JOURNEY
## THROUGH
## DADDY ISSUES

**AUTHOR: P'JAE JARRELL**

INKWORKS

Unraveling Daddy's Shadow :

A Daughter's Journey Through Daddy

Issues

Copyright © 2024 by P'Jae Jarrell

should consult with a professional when appropriate.

To the maximum extent permitted by law, the publisher and the author disclaim any and all liability in the event any information, commentary, analysis, opinions, advice, and/or recommendations contained in this book prove to be inaccurate, incomplete, or unreliable or result in any investment or other losses. Neither the publisher nor the author shall be liable for any loss of profit or any other commercial damages, including but not limited to special, incidental, consequential, personal, or other damages.

For information contact :

pj@pjaejarrell.com

**www.pjaejarrell.com**

Book and Cover design by P'Jae Jarrell

To my two beautiful daughters, who light up my life, and to my mom, my constant guide. This book is for you, my guiding stars.

# Table of CONTENTS

The bond between a father and his daughter is a powerful and intricate connection within the complex web of human relationships. It profoundly impacts a daughter's identity formation and her journey into adulthood. However, for some individuals, this relationship can cause deep emotional distress, commonly referred to as "daddy issues."

We will undertake a journey of understanding, examining the early years of childhood where our relationships with our fathers are formed. We will delve into the various aspects of daddy issues, from the wounds inflicted by absent fathers to the difficulties posed by unhealthy dynamics.

# Chapter 1:
Introduction

These narratives will demonstrate how daddy issues permeate our lives, affecting our self-esteem, trust in others, and relational patterns.

However, this book is not solely focused on pain and struggle. It is a testament to daughters' resilience, healing ability, and growth potential. We will explore the transformative power of self-reflection, therapy, and self-esteem rebuilding. We will emphasize the importance of establishing healthy boundaries and seeking forgiveness for our fathers and ourselves. Through uplifting narratives, we will realize that healing and growth are possible and achievable.

So, join me on this transformative journey as we navigate the depths of daddy issues, unravel our complex experiences, and emerge stronger, wiser, and more complete. Together, we will redefine our narratives, rewrite our stories, and embark on a path of healing, growth, and self-discovery.

## Exploring the Origins

Childhood is the formative stage where the foundations of our personality and relationships are established. It serves as a crucible, molding our perspectives and behaviors based on our experiences, particularly within the family unit. A father and his child share one of the most influential relationships during this stage. This relationship significantly impacts a child's growth, shaping their identity, beliefs, and emotional health.

Exploring the role of fathers in their daughters' lives is like understanding the role of a coach in a sports game. Just as a coach shapes the game's direction with strategies and play calls, a father significantly influences his daughter's life.

Let us dive into what this role entails:

**The Protector:** A dad is often like a safety net for his daughter. Like a coach protects his players, a dad provides security and safety. This makes his daughter feel loved and cared for.

**The Teacher:** Secondly, a dad is like a coach teaching his team the game's rules. He helps his daughter understand important things like honesty, hard work, and respect. He helps her make good decisions and deal with life's challenges.

**The Role Model:** A dad is often the first man in his daughter's life. He sets an example of how men should treat women. This can significantly influence what she expects from men in her future relationships.

Remember, the father-daughter bond is not just about the destination but the journey. It is about the bond that is formed, the protection he provides, the lessons he teaches, the love he shares, and the example he sets, all of which can significantly influence her life. So, let us appreciate and acknowledge the importance of this relationship.

## Defining Daddy Issues

"Daddy issues" is a phrase frequently used in both popular culture and psychological discourse, often carrying with it a certain degree of stigma or negativity. However, to fully comprehend the depth of this term, we need to unpack its true implications. Fundamentally, "daddy issues" encapsulate the range of challenges an individual may encounter because of their relationship, or the absence of it, with their father during their crucial developmental years.

This term is not one-size-fits-all; it reflects various experiences and manifests in multiple ways. Some individuals may grapple with self-esteem issues, continually questioning their worth and value. Others may find it difficult to form and maintain healthy relationships, often due to trust issues or fear of abandonment. Sometimes, the individual may be caught in a relentless pursuit for validation, consciously or unconsciously seeking approval they may not have received from their father figure.

The root of these "daddy issues" can be traced back to various father-daughter dynamics. A father who is absent, either physically or emotionally, can leave a void that the daughter may try to fill throughout her life. Conversely, an overbearing father might lead to feelings of oppression and the need to prove oneself constantly. Similarly, dynamics that are characterized by unhealthy or toxic behaviors can also give rise to these issues. It is important to note that these scenarios are not meant to blame the father figure solely, but to understand the intricate and complex nuances of these relationships that shape an individual's life.

# Chapter 2:

## EXPLORING THE FATHER-DAUGHTER BOND

### The Father-Daughter Dynamic

The Father-Daughter dynamic is a crucial relationship that significantly shapes a girl's life. It is a unique blend of affection, respect, and influence, which plays a vital role in a daughter's development. As the first male figure in a girl's life, a father sets the precedent for how she will perceive men and interact with them throughout her life.

In early childhood, a father is often seen as a protector and provider, a figure of authority and strength. He is the first representation of masculinity a daughter encounters, shaping her understanding of gender roles and expectations. How a father treats his daughter and the women around him can profoundly influence her perception of men.

A respectful, kind, and considerate father can instill in her a healthy expectation of how men should behave. Conversely, if a father is domineering, disrespectful, or abusive, it can warp her perception of men, leading her to expect or accept similar behavior from other men in her life.

Moreover, a father acts as a role model for his daughter. He is the blueprint for her future relationships with men. A daughter's relationship with her father can influence her choice of partner, her expectations from relationships, and her ability to navigate relationship challenges. A daughter who experiences a loving, respectful relationship with her father is more likely to seek out and create similar relationships. On the other hand, a daughter who shares a dysfunctional, unhealthy relationship with her father might struggle with forming healthy relationships, often repeating patterns of dysfunction and conflict.

## Absent Fathers:
## The Impact of Physical or Emotional Absence on a Daughter's Development

The absence of a father, be it physical or emotional, can significantly affect a daughter's development. The term "absent fathers" refers not only to fathers who are physically absent due to death, divorce, or distance but also to those who are physically present but emotionally unavailable.

When a father is physically absent, a daughter may experience feelings of abandonment, rejection, and loss. She may grapple with questions about his absence, often blaming herself for his departure. These feelings can lead to low self-esteem, depression, anxiety, and difficulties in forming healthy relationships. She may also struggle with feelings of insecurity and fear stemming from the absence of a protective figure in her life.

Emotional absence can be equally detrimental even when a father is physically present. A father who is emotionally distant, unresponsive, or neglectful can leave a daughter feeling unseen, unheard, and unimportant. This emotional void can lead to loneliness, unworthiness, and a longing for validation and acceptance. It can also lead to difficulties in understanding and expressing emotions and forming deep connections with others.

Also, the absence of a father can disrupt a daughter's understanding of masculinity and gender roles. Without a positive male figure to learn from, she may develop skewed perceptions of men, often based on negative stereotypes or experiences. This can influence her expectations and experiences in her relationships with men, often leading to patterns of conflict, dissatisfaction, or unfulfilling relationships.

Regarding academic and career development, the absence of a supportive, encouraging figure can undermine a girl's confidence in her abilities and aspirations. It can affect her emotional well-being, her self-esteem, her understanding of gender roles, and her academic and career development.

Recognizing these impacts is crucial, as it can guide interventions and support to mitigate these effects and foster healthy development. However, it is also essential to note that the absence of a father does not doom a daughter to a life of struggle. She can navigate these challenges and thrive with the proper support and resources.

**Overbearing Fathers:**

**Navigating the Challenges of Overprotective or Controlling Fathers'**

Overbearing fathers can present unique challenges for a daughter's development. Often characterized by their overprotective or controlling behaviors, these fathers can unintentionally stifle their daughters' growth and independence.

Overprotective fathers, driven by an intense desire to keep their daughters safe, can inadvertently limit their experiences and opportunities. They may impose strict rules or boundaries, restrict their social interactions, or discourage them from taking risks. While their intentions may be rooted in love and concern, their overprotectiveness can prevent their daughters from learning essential life skills such as problem-solving, decision-making, and risk management.

Controlling fathers, on the other hand, often influence their daughters' choices and actions. They may dictate what their daughters should do, who they should be, or how they should live. This control can undermine their daughters' autonomy and self-confidence, leading to feelings of helplessness, frustration, or resentment. It can also hinder their daughters' ability to assert themselves, express their thoughts and feelings, and make decisions.

Navigating the challenges of overbearing fathers requires a delicate balance of understanding, communication, and assertiveness. Understanding that their overbearing behavior often stems from concern, fear, or insecurity can help daughters empathize with their fathers and not take their behavior personally.

Communication is crucial in addressing these challenges. Open, honest, and respectful conversations about feelings, boundaries, and expectations can clarify misunderstandings, express concerns, and negotiate compromises. Daughters may need to assert their needs and rights, standing up for their independence while acknowledging their fathers' concerns and fears.

## Unhealthy Dynamics:
## Exploring Abusive or Neglectful Relationships and Their Long-term Effects

"Unhealthy dynamics" is a term that can refer to various problematic relationships, including those involving "daddy issues." This term typically refers to difficulties or conflicts in a father-daughter relationship, which can have emotional and psychological implications for the daughter. These issues can stem from witnessing or experiencing the toxic dynamics present in their parent's relationship as well as the father-daughter relationship, which can have deep-seated and long-term effects. When abuse or neglect occurs within these dynamics, it can result in the father being removed from the picture, either physically or emotionally, due to the harm inflicted upon the mother and/or the daughter.

Abusive relationships with a father can manifest in many forms, including physical, emotional, or verbal abuse. This could involve manipulation, verbal insults, violence, or even sexual abuse. These experiences can be incredibly traumatizing, leading to a host of emotional issues, including low self-esteem, depression, anxiety, and post-traumatic stress disorder. The daughter may also struggle with forming healthy relationships, particularly with men, due to fear, distrust, or a skewed perception of how a man should treat her.

Neglectful relationships, on the other hand, are characterized by a father's consistent failure to provide the necessary attention, care, or emotional support.

This could manifest as a father being physically present but emotionally distant or uninvolved in his daughter's life. The impact of such neglect can be just as damaging as abuse. A daughter may develop feelings of unworthiness or invisibility, leading to low self-esteem, difficulties expressing and understanding emotions, and a constant need for validation and approval.

Understanding these unhealthy dynamics and their long-term effects is the first step toward healing. Professional counseling, therapy, or support groups can provide invaluable help in this journey, offering a safe space to process these experiences, learn coping strategies, and rebuild self-esteem.

It is important to remember that while these experiences can shape a person, they do not define them. With the right help and support, individuals can overcome these issues and develop healthy, fulfilling relationships.

# Chapter 3:

## THE PSYCHOLOGICAL IMPACT OF DADDY ISSUES

Understanding the Impact

The influence of 'daddy issues' can be extensive and deeply rooted, affecting various aspects of an individual's life. For some people, a driving force becomes a ceaseless quest for approval, often due to an ingrained sense of inadequacy stemming from an unfulfilled need for paternal validation. This can lead to a pattern of seeking affirmation in unwholesome ways, such as engaging in risky behaviors or forming relationships with individuals who do not respect or value them.

For others, trust issues may arise due to daddy issues. This could result from their father figure's consistent lack of reliability, leading to a deeply ingrained belief that others are unreliable. This often results in difficulties in forming and maintaining healthy and fulfilling relationships.

The psychological impact of "daddy issues" can extend beyond personal relationships and seep into various aspects of one's life, including mental health, academics, and career choices. Daddy issues stemming from an absent, neglectful, or abusive father can create emotional barriers that affect a person's academic performance and career decisions. A supportive father's absence of guidance and validation can lead to self-doubt, low self-esteem, and a fear of failure. This can manifest in academic settings, where individuals with daddy issues may struggle to believe in their abilities or constantly seek external validation. Regarding career choices, the lack of a positive male role model may result in difficulty making confident decisions or setting ambitious goals. The impact of daddy issues on academics and career choices emphasize the importance of providing support, mentorship, and therapeutic interventions to help individuals overcome these psychological hurdles and build a strong foundation for their future success.

Despite the significant impact, these consequences are reasonable. Recognizing and understanding the roots of these 'daddy issues' is critical to healing. It opens the pathway for therapy, self-reflection, and, ultimately, the reclamation of one's self-worth and forming healthier relationships.

## The Importance of Addressing Daddy Issues

Tackling 'daddy issues' is crucial to personal development and establishing wholesome relationships. When left unresolved, these issues can result in cyclical relationship patterns, often forming bonds that mirror the problematic father-child dynamic. Moreover, these issues can distort an individual's perception of their self-worth, often causing them to undervalue themselves and tolerate less than they deserve.

Addressing 'daddy issues' requires the confrontation of uncomfortable memories and emotions. It involves revisiting past traumas, acknowledging the pain, and understanding how these experiences have shaped one's life. While this process is undeniably challenging, it is essential to breaking the cycle of destructive behaviors and relationships. By addressing these issues, individuals can start to reshape their perceptions of self-worth, recognizing that their value is intrinsic and not dependent on external validation. This newfound understanding can lead to healthier relationships where respect, understanding, and love are mutual.

Remember, this part of the journey involves confronting painful truths and enduring emotional discomfort. However, while arduous, this path is one of the most rewarding journeys an individual can undertake. It enables individuals to break free from the shackles of their past and paves the way for personal growth, self-acceptance, and emotional healing.

Healing and growth from daddy issues is a journey of self-discovery, emotional processing, and the development of healthier interpersonal relationships. This path requires courage, resilience, and, often, external support from professionals, such as therapists and counselors.

The first step towards healing is acknowledgment. It involves understanding the impact of the past, the nature of the unhealthy father-daughter dynamic, and how it has affected one's view of oneself and others. This step may be painful, as it entails revisiting traumatic memories and feelings of neglect or abuse. However, acknowledgment is crucial because it provides a clear starting point for moving forward.

Next, emotional processing is vital in the healing journey. This involves expressing and managing the emotions associated with daddy issues, such as anger, sadness, or fear, and remembering that all feelings are valid and that it is okay not to be okay. Therapy can provide a safe and supportive environment for this emotional processing, helping individuals understand and cope with their feelings.

Alongside emotional processing, cognitive restructuring can also be beneficial. This process involves changing the unhealthy beliefs or thoughts one might have developed due to daddy issues. For instance, a daughter might believe that she is unworthy of love or that all men are untrustworthy. Cognitive restructuring helps to replace these negative beliefs with healthier, more balanced ones.

The development of healthier relationships is another critical aspect of healing and growth. This can involve setting boundaries, improving communication, and building trust with others. It can also mean learning to seek and develop relationships with people who treat you kindly and respectfully.

Lastly, self-care and self-love are central to healing from daddy issues. This involves caring for your physical, emotional, and mental health and learning to love and accept yourself. It is about understanding that the past does not define one's worth or by others' actions or opinions.

Healing and growth from daddy issues can be a very challenging journey. However, the journey can also be filled with potential for personal transformation and empowerment. It is a learning journey to let go of the past, embrace the present, and move towards a healthier, happier future. Remember, there is no set timeline for healing, and seeking help and support along the way is okay.

**Awareness and Self-reflection:**

**Recognizing the Presence and Impact of Daddy Issues**

In the journey towards healing, you must embark on a path of self-discovery, awareness, and reflection. When addressing daddy issues, being aware of their presence and understanding their impact is a crucial first step. Through self-reflection, individuals can navigate the intricate layers of these issues and pave the way for healing and personal growth.

Awareness is the key that unlocks the door to transformation. It involves recognizing and acknowledging the presence of daddy issues in one's life. By becoming aware of their existence, individuals can understand how these issues have influenced their thoughts, emotions, and behaviors.

Self-reflection plays a vital role in the healing process. It involves looking inward, examining one's experiences, and understanding how daddy issues have shaped one's perspective. Through self-reflection, individuals can uncover deep-seated emotions, patterns, and beliefs influenced by their relationship with their father. This process allows for a deeper understanding of oneself and the impact of daddy issues on various aspects of life.

It is essential to approach self-reflection with kindness and compassion during the healing process. Exploring deep-rooted emotions and painful memories can be challenging. However, by embracing self-compassion and practicing self-care, individuals can create a safe and nurturing environment for healing. Seeking support from trusted friends, family members, or professionals can provide guidance and a listening ear throughout this journey.

Awareness and self-reflection also open the door to breaking the cycle of unhealthy patterns and behaviors. By understanding how daddy issues have influenced choices in relationships, career paths, and personal growth, individuals gain the power to make conscious decisions that align with their true desires and values. They can set boundaries, establish healthier connections, and pursue their dreams with a newfound sense of clarity and purpose.

## Seeking therapy:
## The Benefits of Professional Guidance in Addressing and Resolving Deep-Rooted Issues

Addressing and resolving daddy issues can be a complex process. Professional guidance through therapy or counseling can provide the necessary tools and support to navigate this journey more effectively. Therapists can help to unpack traumatic experiences, challenge unhealthy belief systems, and facilitate the development of healthier coping mechanisms. Yes, I have been there!

One of the most common therapeutic approaches used to address daddy issues is Cognitive-Behavioral Therapy (CBT). CBT focuses on identifying and challenging distorted thought patterns and beliefs, which often stems from past traumatic experiences. The goal is to replace these harmful thoughts with healthier ones, promoting positive feelings and behaviors. For instance, a therapist might help a daughter challenge the belief that she is unlovable due to her father's neglect and replace it with the understanding that she is inherently worthy of love and respect.

Psychodynamic therapy is another approach that can be beneficial. This therapy focuses on uncovering unconscious thoughts and emotions that influence behavior. It emphasizes exploring past experiences, particularly those from childhood, to understand how they have shaped current behaviors and attitudes. In the context of daddy issues, a psychodynamic therapist might help a daughter explore her past relationship with her father and how it has influenced her self-perception and relationships.

Trauma-focused therapy can be particularly beneficial for those who have experienced traumatic experiences with their fathers. These therapies aim to help individuals process and make sense of their traumatic experiences, reducing their impact on current life.

However, finding a qualified therapist who specializes in working with father-daughter relationships is critical. A therapist with this specialization will better understand these relationships' unique dynamics and challenges. They can provide targeted interventions that facilitate healing and growth.

**Rebuilding Self-Esteem:**
**Strategies for Developing a Positive Self-Image and Overcoming Insecurities**

Rebuilding self-esteem after experiencing daddy issues is a transformative process that requires patience, dedication, and a deep understanding of one's worth. It involves replacing negative self-beliefs with positive ones, practicing self-care, and fostering self-compassion.

Self-esteem is a reflection of how one perceives oneself. It influences our thoughts, emotions, and behaviors, shaping our interactions with others and the world. When daddy issues lead to diminished self-esteem, daughters often struggle with feelings of worthlessness, insecurity, and self-doubt.

The first step in rebuilding self-esteem is to challenge and replace negative self-beliefs. These beliefs might include thoughts such as "I am unlovable" or "I am not good enough." Recognizing these thoughts as distortions of reality, influenced by past experiences, and not reflective of one's true worth is essential. Cognitive restructuring, a psychological technique that involves identifying and challenging negative thoughts, can be particularly beneficial here. Replacing these harmful beliefs with positive affirmations can gradually build a healthier self-image.

Self-care also plays a pivotal role in rebuilding self-esteem. This involves caring for one's physical, emotional, and mental health. It can include exercising regularly, eating healthily, getting adequate sleep, practicing mindfulness or engaging in hobbies. By taking care of oneself, one indirectly communicates the message: "I am worthy of care and attention," which can significantly boost self-esteem.

Moreover, fostering self-compassion is crucial in this journey. Self-compassion entails being kind and understanding towards you, especially during times of failure or when confronting personal flaws. It is about accepting yourself unconditionally, imperfections and all. Self-compassion allows you to view mistakes and failures as opportunities for growth rather than reflections of your worth.

Rebuilding self-esteem from daddy issues is not an overnight process. It requires time, patience, and consistent effort. It might also involve seeking professional help, such as therapy or counseling, to navigate this journey effectively. However, daughters become more resilient with each step towards a healthier self-image and embrace their inherent value, leading to a more fulfilling and empowered life.

**Establishing Healthy Boundaries:**
**Learning to Set Boundaries in Relationships and Prioritize Self-Care When Healing**

Practical boundary setting is fundamental to developing healthy relationships and promoting personal well-being, especially when healing from daddy issues. It involves defining acceptable behavior towards you and what is not, enabling you to protect your emotional and mental health.

Your boundaries are deeply personal, influenced by your values, past experiences, and current needs. Depending on the context, these boundaries can be physical, emotional, or mental. For instance, a physical boundary might involve not wanting to be touched without consent. In contrast, a moving boundary might involve not tolerating disrespectful or disparaging comments.

Assertive communication is vital when setting boundaries. It requires clearly and respectfully expressing your needs and expectations to others. Being strong does not mean being aggressive or confrontational; instead, it is about standing up for oneself calmly and confidently. For instance, if a father's criticism is causing distress, an assertive response might be, "I understand that you have concerns, but I need you to express them more respectfully."

However, setting boundaries is only half the task.

Maintaining them consistently is equally essential. This involves reinforcing your boundaries when crossed and taking necessary actions, such as distancing yourself from individuals who always disrespect your boundaries. It is necessary to remember that you have a right to protect your mental and emotional well-being, even if it means upsetting others or causing temporary discomfort.

Prioritizing self-care is another crucial part of this process. Self-care involves taking care of one's physical, emotional, and mental health. It could include eating healthily, exercising regularly, practicing mindfulness, or engaging in joyous hobbies. By prioritizing self-care, you communicate to yourself and others that your needs and well-being are essential, bolstering your confidence in maintaining your boundaries.

Establishing healthy boundaries is empowering. It fosters self-respect, improves relationships, and creates a healthier balance in one's life. Furthermore, it provides a sense of control, allowing you to navigate your journey of healing from daddy issues more safely and confidently.

**Forgiveness and Acceptance:**

**Finding Closure and Moving Forward by Reconciling with Past Traumas**

Forgiveness and acceptance are potent tools in the process of healing, particularly from the pain and trauma associated with daddy issues. This process often involves reconciling with past hurts, acknowledging their impact, and letting go of the anger and resentment that can keep us emotionally entangled.

Forgiveness, in this context, does not mean condoning or forgetting the painful actions or behavior of one's father. Instead, it is about acknowledging the hurt, releasing the emotional burden, and choosing not to let past mistakes define oneself or their future relationships. It is essential to understand that forgiveness is for the individual, not the person who caused the pain. It allows one to reclaim power, paving the way for emotional freedom and personal growth.

Forgiving a father for his shortcomings, mistakes, or absence can be challenging and may take time. It is a personal journey that requires patience, courage, and self-compassion. One might start by acknowledging their hurt and anger, then gradually work towards understanding and empathy, perhaps by considering the father's limitations, struggles, or past traumas. This is not to excuse harmful behavior but to provide a broader perspective that can help in forgiveness.

However, in addition to forgiving others, self-forgiveness is equally critical. Often, individuals grappling with daddy issues may blame themselves for their strained relationship with their father or repeated patterns in their relationships. It is essential to recognize that the actions of others, particularly parents, do not reflect one's worth or lovability. Self-forgiveness involves letting go of this self-blame and accepting oneself, flaws, and all.

Acceptance is the next step in this journey. It involves acknowledging one's past experiences, accepting them as part of one's story, but not allowing them to dictate their future. Acceptance does not mean resignation; it is about recognizing reality and choosing to move forward despite it.

# Chapter 5:

## REDEFINING
## RELATIONSHIPS

**Building Healthy Connections with Others and Partners**

Healing from daddy issues is like finishing a complex puzzle. Once you have completed it, you are ready to start a new puzzle; this time, you are better prepared. You can apply what you learned to redefine relationships and build healthier connections with others, partners, and yourself. Here is how you can do it:

**With Partners: Building a healthy relationship with a partner is like working on a puzzle together. You must communicate effectively, respect each other's boundaries, and show empathy. It is about working together to build a strong and healthy connection.

**With Others:** Think of each person as a unique puzzle piece. You need to understand each piece to see where it fits. It is about understanding what each person brings to your life and how you can work together to create a beautiful picture.

Remember, redefining your relationships is not about making everything perfect. It is about making things healthier and happier. It is about learning from your past and using it to create a better future. Moreover, just like a puzzle, it might take time and patience. However, once it is complete, you can step back and appreciate the beautiful picture you have created.

## Creating Healthy Connections with Fathers

Healing from daddy issues is like mending a broken bridge. Once fixed, you can cross over to a land of authentic connections. This means creating genuine, honest relationships with your dad. Let us look at how you can cross that bridge after healing:

**\*\*Effective Communication:**
It is like a bridge that can help you cross a river of misunderstandings and hurt feelings. It is about speaking your truth clearly and listening to your dad's truth, too. Remember, a conversation is a two-way street. It is about understanding and being understood. Let us talk about how you can build that bridge:

**Express Your Needs:**

This is about telling your dad what you need from him. You may need him to listen more or to be more understanding. It is essential to be transparent and honest about these needs. Remember, your dad cannot read your mind. If you do not tell him what you need, he might not know.

**Set Clear Expectations:**

This is about letting your dad know what you expect from him. For example, let him know if you want him to be more supportive. Be specific about what that support looks like. Again, be honest and transparent.

**Practice Active Listening:**

This means paying attention to what your dad is saying, not just waiting for your turn to speak. It is about showing him that his feelings and thoughts matter to you.

**\*\*Empathy:**

This is like the support beams of the bridge. It holds up the structure. It is about feeling your dad's feelings and helping him feel what you feel. Empathy can build a more profound and stronger connection, making the bridge sturdier.

**\*\*Setting Boundaries:**

This is like the guardrails of the bridge. They keep you safe as you cross. It is about deciding what is okay and not okay in your relationship with your dad. It may not be okay for him to criticize you all the time. Alternatively, it is not okay for him to ignore your feelings. It is essential to be clear about these boundaries and to communicate them to your dad. It is about creating a safe space where your connection can grow.

**\*\*Maintaining Boundaries:**

Setting boundaries is one thing but keeping them is another. This might mean reminding your dad about the boundaries if he forgets. Alternatively, it could mean standing your ground even if it feels uncomfortable. Remember, it is okay to protect your emotional well-being.

**Mutual Respect and Understanding:**

This is like the road on the bridge. It is what you walk on as you cross. It is about treating each other with kindness and respect. It is about listening to each other's thoughts and feelings and not doing or saying things to hurt each other. It is about understanding each other's needs and feelings. Remember, respect is a two-way street. You deserve respect; showing respect to your dad is also important.

**Healthy Dynamics:**

This is about creating a positive and healthy relationship with your dad. It is about finding a balance between your needs and his. It is about working together to solve problems and respect each other's boundaries.

Remember, creating an authentic connection with your dad is a journey. It can take time and patience. However, you can find a genuine, honest, and strong relationship once you cross that bridge. Moreover, that can be a beautiful thing.

# Chapter 6:

EMPOWERING NARRATIVES

Breaking the Cycle:
Empowering Daughters to Create Positive Legacies
for Future Generations

When we talk about "daddy issues," we are often talking about problems that can continue from one generation to the next. It is like a spinning wheel, repeatedly causing the same issues. However, here is the good news: that wheel can be stopped. It is all about breaking the cycle and creating a better story for yourself and future generations.

So, how do you break the cycle?

**Understand the Past: The first step is understanding the cycle. This means looking back at your relationship with your dad and maybe even your relationship with his dad. It is not about blaming anyone but understanding why things happened the way they did.

**\*\*Make a Change:** Once you understand the cycle, you can plan to change it. This might mean standing up for yourself, setting stronger boundaries, or getting help from a counselor or therapist. Remember, it is okay to ask for help.

**\*\*Believe in Yourself:** This is crucial. You must believe that you can break the cycle. You must believe you are strong, intelligent, and brave enough to make a change.

When you break the cycle, you are helping yourself and the people who come after you. You may have a daughter someday or be a role model for other girls. By breaking the cycle, you show them they can do the same. Breaking the cycle is not about forgetting the past. It is about learning from it, growing stronger, and creating a better future. It is about turning "daddy issues" into a story of strength, courage, and empowerment. Moreover, that is a story worth telling.

## Sharing Personal Stories:
## Real-life Experiences of Daughters Overcoming Daddy Issues

As we journey deeper into the heart of healing, we now arrive at a space of raw honesty and palpable emotion. The next part of my book is dedicated to the real-life experiences of daughters overcoming daddy issues. These are tales of resilience, strength, and unwavering hope. These are short stories of real women who, like many of us, have grappled with the pain of a strained father-daughter relationship. They have bravely navigated the tumultuous waters of healing and emerged with newfound wisdom and understanding. Though deeply personal and unique, their journeys offer a beacon of light for those still navigating their way out of the darkness.

As you read the stories, remember that each one is a testament to the power of transformation and the human spirit's capacity to overcome:

### "Overcoming My Past" by Jazmine B.

Jazmine had always struggled with a sense of abandonment due to her father's absence during her childhood. After years of therapy, she realized that she had been seeking validation and love from others, mirroring the void left by her father. Jazmine shares her journey of forgiveness, saying, "I realized that my father was a flawed human too, dealing with his issues. By forgiving him, I released the anger that was holding me back. It did not happen overnight, but I felt lighter, more in control of my life."

**"Breaking the Cycle" by Jenny M.**

Jenny grew up in a home where her father was emotionally unavailable. This led her to form relationships where she felt the same sense of emotional neglect. Through personal growth and therapy, she learned to set healthy boundaries. She said, "I used to let people treat me poorly at my job and in relationships, thinking that was all I deserved. However, I have learned to value myself and set boundaries. I will not accept less than respect and love."

**"A Journey to Self-Love" by Sade J.**

Sade's father was overly critical, leading Sade to develop a harsh inner critic. After years of battling low self-esteem, she shares her turning point: "I realized that I had internalized my father's voice calling me incompetent, constantly criticizing myself. I learned to replace that voice with one of love and acceptance. It was hard, but it has been the most liberating experience of my life."

### "Finding Forgiveness" by Jessica M.

Jessica's father was never there for her growing up, causing her to feel abandoned. Over time, she came to understand that her father was dealing with his issues-drugs, toxic women, and career struggles because he had made bad decisions growing up and having to be the man of the house at a young age. Jessica writes, "I decided to forgive him. Not because he deserved it, but because I deserved peace."

### "My Journey Towards Self-Worth" by Tisa D.

Tisa had a father who was constantly belittling her and appearing in her life at his convenience, not when she needed him. This led to a pattern of self-doubt and low self-esteem. With therapy, Tisa learned to value herself. She shares, "I have had to work hard to silence the negative voice in my head, the one echoing my father's words and actions. However, now, I know his opinions do not define my worth."

## "Breaking Free" by Latoyia H.

Latoyia's father was emotionally abusive, which led her to seek out similar relationships in her adulthood. If a guy did not show aggression and maybe even dominance/control, she felt he did not love her or was considered lame. After recognizing the pattern, Latoyia chose to break the cycle. She shares, "I realized I deserved more than my father had shown me. So, I began setting boundaries for myself and others, which has been a game-changer for my mental health."

These stories remind us that while the journey may be challenging, it is empowering and transformative.

**"My Story Amidst Our Collective Healing" by P'Jae J.**

My journey began in the absence of a traditional father figure, with my father passing away when I was just 11 months old. The void he left was immense, but it was lovingly filled by the first man I ever loved, my grandfather. He affectionately dubbed me "Papa's Queen," treating me with kindness and reverence that set the foundation for how I expected to be treated by men in my life. My grandfather was my protector, my confidante, and my guiding star.

He shielded me from the quarrels with my older cousins and made me feel like royalty. Every day with him was an adventure, whether it was a simple trip to the grocery store with him and my grandma or listening intently to his passionate sermons at church.

But this sense of security and love was abruptly taken from me at the tender age of five when I found him unresponsive in our home. The loss was devastating, a wound made deeper by my young mind's inability to fully grasp that I would never again share those precious moments with him.

In the wake of his passing, the mantle of male influence in my life was passed to my eldest Uncle. As time went on, my mom married and I gained a stepfather, but we struggled to find common ground, especially with his busy schedule balancing Army Reserve duties and two jobs. Thankfully, my male cousins, especially Alton, stepped in. Through them, I learned about the multifaceted nature of masculinity, discovering that not all men are the same. Despite the common refrain that men are logical, I observed a broad spectrum of thoughts, feelings, and behaviors among them. This exposure shaped my understanding of men and influenced my expectations in relationships.

Growing up, I yearned for the "Queen treatment" I had come to know — a relationship filled with protection, chivalry, unwavering support, romance, and surprises. While many of my long-term relationships did provide this to some extent, there always seemed to be something missing, an elusive piece that kept the picture from being complete.

In the midst of navigating my tangled web of daddy issues and the intricate dynamics of male relationships in my life, I found solace and clarity in therapy. This journey into the depths of my psyche was not an easy one, but it was necessary for my healing. Therapy provided me with a safe space to unpack the layers of grief, loss, and longing that had accumulated since my father's death and my grandfather's passing. It was here that I learned the invaluable lesson that healing is not a destination but a continuous process.

As I continue to write my story, both literally and metaphorically, journaling remains a cornerstone of my healing process. It is a reminder that while the wounds of the past may never entirely disappear, their hold on me weakens with each word I write. Through the combined power of therapy and journaling, I am not just surviving; I am thriving, rewriting the narrative of my life one day at a time.

Determined not to let the cycle continue, I've engaged in open and honest conversations with my children about self-love, boundaries, leadership, self-care, self-worth, and respect. They've witnessed both the beauty of a successful co-parenting relationship and the pain of two people in love growing apart. Through these experiences, I've aimed to teach them the importance of communication and understanding in all relationships.

Healing from Daddy's Issues is like finishing an intense and challenging book. You have turned the last page, but the story does not end there. It is time to start a new book, a new narrative, and this one is all about self-discovery and the exciting possibilities that lie ahead. Let us explore what this new narrative can look like:

**Self-Discovery:

This is like the introduction of your new book. It is about getting to know the main character – YOU. It is about understanding your feelings, your needs, and your strengths. It is about discovering who you are and who you want to become.

# Chapter 7:
## Embracing A New Narrative

## **New Possibilities:

This is like the plot of your new book. It is about exploring all the exciting things that can happen now that you have healed from your daddy issues. It is about setting new goals, trying new things, and building healthier relationships with others.

## **Embracing Change:

This is like the theme of your new book. It is about accepting that change is a part of life and learning to embrace it. It is about knowing that it is okay to grow and change and that it is never too late to start a new chapter.

As you close this book, remember that your story does not end here. It is just the beginning of a new narrative, a new journey of self-discovery and new possibilities. Moreover, just like any good book, it will be filled with twists and turns. However, the rest is still to be written, and you are holding the pen. You have the power to write a story full of love, respect, and positivity. So, with each page you turn, you will grow stronger, wiser, and happier. Embrace your new narrative and look forward to all the beautiful things ahead. This is your story.